the whole mad swirl of everything to come begins now!

What's New
Poetry Forum
Short Stories
Mad Gallery
Open Mic
Submissions

Sam Silva
SPRING SINGS SILLY HAIKU
featured in the poetry forum June 5, 2022 :: 0 comments

hear the water lap
the shores of the melted lake
...with only kisses
editors note:

You'll need a towel after that kiss and cuddle. – mh clay
LYNN SHARE HAIKU
featured in the poetry forum March 27, 2022 :: 0 comments

pain and anxiety
over the telephone line
step by step resolved
editors note:

Everyone is looking for a Lynn to lighten the load. – mh clay
2 Haiku: THE FROST OF DAWN & TREES
featured in the poetry forum January 16, 2022 :: 0 comments

THE FROST OF DAWN

silently cold comes
against the blues of friday
...love, lonely sinking

***

TREES

nature breathes, sweats rain
I am in awe by window
views of my garden
editors note:

Outer spaces spur inner graces. – mh clay

Three Haiku: Sale, Lucky, Gnats
featured in the poetry forum October 21, 2021 :: 0 comments

THE SALE

this huge house I love
...this relic of a small past
...away and gone now

***
LUCKY GUY

I was luckiest
when things fell apart. The world
baked like dough to bread

***
GNATS

gnats swarm in the sun
the day is itchy rotten
the apple stinks too much
editors note:

Just as life comes in short bursts; our luck can turn on the sale of a gnat. – mh clay
LIGHT HAIKU
featured in the poetry forum July 19, 2021 :: 0 comments

a light diffuses black
..it lathers the sky that way
...clouds spread like thunder
editors note:

A light lather is a close shave. – mh clay
FRANKENSTEIN
featured in the poetry forum April 30, 2021 :: 0 comments

Places where the dead are plugged
...electric to all passion's core
wandering the peasant groves
...confused by an uncertain brain
and terrorizing man and beast
and women also
like a boar
searching warmth
in fear of fire.
Destruction in desire's feast
the way the dead can feel desire!!

editors note:

Like this, we grope our grove, in search of life's bright bolt. – mh clay
LIVING AMONG THE MIDDLE CLASSES
featured in the poetry forum February 2, 2021 :: 0 comments

An achy nervousness
among pandemic days
while summer turns toward Fall
and the politics of madness
in the election of it all

and my own old age decays
dully for its sadness
like some disease which slays

with a sleep that fills our eyes
with an image on TV
of dreamy dreamy hot fires
in the skies.
editors note:

Flat screen, flat deal! We are what we watch. – mh clay
THE LOVE BOND
featured in the poetry forum November 7, 2020 :: 0 comments

See we are ancient already! We are marble
carved and sealed to fortressed stone
inseparable the way we aged together
and glistening in our polish
like one of your starry paintings.

Or an old rustic house
grown out as one toward the woodland.
We live in the same skin
shelter under each other's locks.

I look out the window of your brilliant eyes
and see and give utterance for the world
eternally brand new!
editors note:

Yes! Give utterance! – mh clay
THE FAILED ARTIST
featured in the poetry forum August 17, 2020 :: 0 comments

Nature's first rule is predation
a fact in the face

which he could not stand

so he puffed up a cloud
in his glacial station
to obscure that cruel beauty
of the land.
editors note:

In this case, smoke 'em when you DON'T... – mh clay
ART AS THE GHOSTLY SOPRANO
featured in the poetry forum June 15, 2020 :: 0 comments

This is the love among the dead
...these are those high operatic notes
...that gorge of meat and wine and bread
...that private castle leaking hope, despair,
the two the same in desperate sighs

encased in predatory motes
to keep away the warlike herds
of Mongols milking mares and goats
with lost dreams much like lullabies
composed by angels

....without words...
editors note:

And, yet, we must sing them... – mh clay

   1
   2
   3
   ?

A bit about Sam: Sam Silva has poetry in print magazines including, but not limited to Samisdat, The ECU Rebel, Sow's Ear, The American Muse, St. Andrews Review, Dog River Review, Third Lung Review, Main St. Rag, Charlotte Poetry Review, Parnasus...most (but not all) of these magazines are now defunct. For the past four years his magazine portfolio has grown by and large on line including Rio Del Arts, Megaera, Big Bridge, Views unplugged, Comrade Magazine, Ken Again and at least thirty others. Over the years four small presses have published a total of nine chapbooks by Sam Silva ...these, being Third Lung Press, M.A.F. Press, Alpha Beat Press, Trouth Creek Press. Brown and Yale Universities solicited many of these chapbooks for their libraries. These chapbooks were well received in newspaper reviews by Shelby Stephenson, Ron Bayes, Steve Smith, and the late poet laureate of North Carolina Sam Ragan. Silva has ebooks available without cost at Physikgarden.com. He has well over 300 poems archived in online magazines. He was nominated a total of seven times by three small presses and has a full length collection of poetry called Eating and Drinking based on a royalties contract signed with Bright Spark Creative available for order at any online bookstore and has other full length poetry books

available at amazon.com. Three spoken word CDs of Sam Silva's have been marketed through
CDBaby.

What's New
Poetry
Short Stories
Mad Gallery
Open Mic
The Best of Mad Swirl
Mad Reviews
Merch
Submissions
Contact

EVEN WITH CLIMATE CHANGE HAIKU

the days are still flush
with shivering spring again
the days go cooly

STUPID ME HAIKU

i stumble these days
wait stupidly to die here
happy i am now

UNLUCKY SPRING HAIKU

the days pass from dawn
till the music of nighttime
i hum poems waiting

THE MARROW BLEEDS TO SEED HAIKU

waking slowly now
a third time in the morning
over a cup of brew

SPRING LULLABY HAIKU

the days warn slowly
even now from chill to heat
the porch is stunning

MARCH 25TH HAIKU

the warm sunlight creeps
through morning portals it flows
to the forest floor

LOVE AND NATURE

these broken twigs show
the rustic signs of my heart
...my love is wooded

COUNTRY GIRL HAIKU

you are sweetest song
heart of the farm and forest
for you i live, die

SPRING SINGS SILLY HAIKU

hear the water lap
the shores of the melted lake
....with only kisses

BRSK LOGIC HAIKU

one step at a time
toward where the bottom leads to
at the end of it

BRISK NONSENSE HAIKU

walk rapidly nowhere
on nothingness crazy sore

with memories gone

SPRING SHIVERS HAIKU

early dawn we wake
the sunlight creeps upon us
outside the porch door

WINDMILLS HAIKU

windmills make movement
for power from the ocean
far out in the waves

THE PROBLEM HAIKU

i was born wrongly

some part of me was dumb then
...unable to speak

WHAT STRANGE THING HAIKU

what strange thing was it?
that caused my collapse these years
...strange thing forgotten

I AM HAPPY HAIKU

i am happy now
live well with my confusion
in this strange country

THE TRAGIC HEART LAUGHS HAIKU

here in old age laugh
like us god laughs just as well
all night by the fire

EACH BLADE OF GRASS HAIKU

life and death in each
in each stringy blade of grass
...stand up and laugh now

JOY HAIKU

music and nature
fill the world the trees, oceans
flood my heart with love

DESCENT HAIKU

down we went enjoined
to the basement of our love
to stare at ourselves

FRONTAL LABOTOMY HAIKU

as i age dull mind
i grow pacific inside
...waddle in the sun

WE SMILE ACHING HAIKU

laughter falls upon us
with our pain...is part of age
this way of our lives

PUSHING LIKE NAKED SPRING HAIKU

root to bud this time
innocent and stubbornly
i fallow downward

THE STUPID WAYS WE LOVE HAIKU

simple and singular
dully straight toward your heart
i give you my gift

STILL SHIVERIG HAIKU

winter keeps a cold
eye on the paths that i take
blows to let me know

SEEDS HAIKU

they are put away
in the soil and forgotten
until fall darkens

AFTERNOON HAIKU

the hot buttery
sunlight of a late mid-spring day
made me so sleepy

APRIL IS A CURSE HAIKU

april is a curse
made to crucify small gods
..weak, they drown always

NAKED REMNANTS HAIKU

not from the bath but
from winter's trees clawing out
the earth in springtime

STEWING HAIKU

only music calms
in this cycle of pure nerves
no cigarettes now

DAYS OF WONDERFUL NOTHIING HAIKU

nothing happens now
...this day yawns and streches out
like a fat balloon

EASING CLOUDY HAIKU

it looks to be rain
this pain of our struggling
underneath the sky

TEARS OF APRIL HAIKU

april rains in earnest
weeps like a mourning mother
all day long today

THE HARBOR OF MY HEART HAIKU

she who swells embracing
me and joking like smoke, fire,
...we laugh eternal

ANGELS RISE HAIKU

we see them streak up
like fire in the night they rise
while we watch sitting

SIGHS OF APRIL HAIKU

easter blesses us
the god who would return and
seek us in the flesh

HUMAN PIG HAIKU

the dire sense of night
...two a.m. and jam and toast
...the belly swells up

HUMAN PIG 2 HAIKU

wishing the fat would
melt away at two a.m.
...a sick way to die

HUMAN PIG 3 HAIKU

stareing at the black
pit of our dreams much like pork
roasting on a skewer

TREPIDATIONS HAIKU

Spring seems to be slow
the death of global warming
we   aimless wander

THE BEAUTY OF THE DEAD HAIKU

We are so human
tragiically woven the way
...there is no other

MY LOVER SHOULD LIVE HAPPY HAIKU

and her children also
she is more precious than these
useless tears we weep

HAPPY AND DEPRESSED HAIKU

we move slowly now
laughing moodily at dry
facts as they approach

THE HOURS ARE LONG AND SHORT HAIKU

long hours pass..we wait
for some sudden tradgedy
there are manny now

THE MIND KNOWS HOPE HAIKU

although. senselessly
we destroy our future, we
do not beilve it

REPUBLICANS HAIKU

fascists junk the earth
the planet is their garbage
nature dies...kills them

REPUBLICANS 2 HAIKU

the earth is a meal
made for the fat and greedy
they eat it and die

REPUBLICANS 3 HAIKU

bit coin rules the world
destroys it with methane too
we are rich with death

BREAKDOWN HAIKU

car trouble came on
a few days ago with us
cabin bound we are

BREAKDOWN 2 Haiku

my mnd is squeezed here
i pace the floors neurotic
...tense i pace the floors

BREAKDOWN 3 HAIKU

at night i am scarred
by the way the world goes on
sleep less...pace the floors

LONG PANTS IN SPRING HAIKU

morning is still cold
i shiver on the porch chair
stare off distantly

WORRYING TOO MUCH HAIKU

things are bad on earth
wars and climate change as well
...i crawl into shade

NERVOUS SLEEPNG HAIKU

i am barely awke
in the midst of dreaming on
nightmares...sick ending

NERVOUS SLEEPING 2 HAIKU

instead i am woke
but miserabley so this time
...opiim seems nice

NERVOUS SLEEPING 3 HAIKU

shallow sleep snoring
in the pit of my stomach
while i wish to drowse

END OF THE WORLD HAIKU

war, pestilence, plague
flood and drought as well begin
too fast...the ways down

END OF THE WORLD 2 HAIKU

but this has happened
before and too much again
nobody believes

STARE AT THE TV HAIKU

boring distractions
and the horror showas well
it could be blankness

HOWEVER LONG HAIKU

however long we
last, let us love forever
with our kiss and sigh

NATURE STIILL CALMS HAIKU

the waterfalls sound
...the wind touches us as well
.....things are brief, easy

BRIEF AND EASY HAIKU

I do weep for loss
but have little more to do
beside my vote now

GOOD FRIDAYING HAIKU

nails and shivering
terror matched by pain as well
and abandonment

GRAY GHOST OF SATURDAY HAIKU

the deep pit of sleep
surrounds of every intent
...piteous sleep too

THE EASTER OF EVERYTHING HAIKU

this is all of it
this is the tomb of jesus
our halelujahs

PORCUPINE HAIKU

hungry and numb here
...i swell in the belly's grip
inhaling food stuffs

PORCUPINE 2 HAIKU

my needles are sharo
but insciincually poised
to stupidly strike

PORCUPINE 3 HAIKU

i am used to it
indifferant now i munch
peaefully of food

THE END HAIKU

i try to eat less

drink and smoke nothing as well
nature is gorgeous

THE END 2 HAIKU

there may be war now
for all of us on the earth
at such a harsh time

THE END 3 HAIKU

we warm to a flood
we burn to a fire as well
in these fat days now

WHEN WE DIE HAIKU

when we pass does the
ghost of our ashes rise up
to god like a kiss

WHEN WE DIE 2 HAIKU

i hope my lover
will live forever she is
so good and sweet too

WHEN WE DIE 3 HAIKU

we are dust, trembling
in a bin and spill to mix
with the waters here

SPRING DAYS HAIKU

april has born light
on wooded acres in the day
and tvs at night

SPRING DAYS 2 HAIKU

trying to thin down
as the warm days come to us
sitting on a porch

SPRING DAYS 3 HAIKU

things are beautiful
as they disappear with heat
...coal and oil burning

RAPID FIRE HAIKU

machine guns rattle
nerves fly in the kitchen of
my hungry eating

RAPID FIRE 2 HAIKU

machine guns firing
bombs blasting orphans' mothers
the fascist onslaught

RAPID FIRE 3 HAIKU

stuccato bullets
in air void of life, and so
winning seems empty

FAKE NEWS HAIKU

there is no war there
civilian deaths are a lie!
...russia denies this

FAKE NEWS 2 HAIKU

republicans too
deny bidens election
likewise is unreal

FAKE NEWS 3 HAIKU

there is no warming
there is such denial these days
we die in comfort

HAIKU c

HAIKU 1c

these stars tumble down
when the earth warms up to this
ending of all things

HAIKU 2c

the word kills me now
from the time i was born here
the word comes to kill

HAIKU 2c

such sad facts we are
we struggle with opinions
on our comming deaths

3 JOKE HAIKU

a wink and a dive
and the world is quickly gone
down in the sewer

terror rips at us
we feel its deadly clawing
on our skins sinking

i wish i could sleep
inside this chaos around
never feel it at all

2 NATURE HAIKU

under day's dim haze
pedestrians force theselves
to walk unhidden

tenderly go there
to the circle of flowers
surrounding us too

3 NATURE HAIKU

light covers nature
in the swamp of our garden
...goes into the depths

4 CITY HAIKU

septic! you know stench
smells like famaldahide
just like the rest do

americans are
fat from medical problems
like eating too much

NATURE 3 HAIKU

angry birds, brilliant
in their dawn display of song
give grace to the world

a deep view of things
like my love for rachels warmth
...so intenesely true

the cunt of our love
the flower of our being
crazy and intense

SADLY THE DARK GREEN; TWO HAIKU

sadly the dark green
lies naked in the morning
deep beyond my porch

the heart from summer
so lively in the past times
has now ruined us

THREE HAIKU FOR DESPAIR

sighs from the blither
at the bottom...that crap of all
endings sinking down

terror and reasonless

despair in such things as pull
us from sleeping on

crown of all headaches
yawn of the chasm in us
days when the earth warms

DULL THE DARK DAY HAIKU

dull the dark morning
dreadfull numb shiver away
from the hopelessness

slip into shiver
dark morning tremble of cool
fear of the nighttime

INDOOR HAIKU

headache of the cool
airconditioned ambience
slipping into spring

WAITING FOR THE WEEKEND HAIKU

the music comes friday
on the lovely radio
still getting hot here

THE VIEW HAIKU

nature loves my pain
essence and release of me
in milky morning

THE INFERNO HAIKU

the stench and evil
of hell bleeds from this poet
in redemption still

these are the things come
purify the marred and tired
soul of ours at dawn

NATURE HEART HAIKU

we wound nature now
...the gulls cry out mournfully
...the icebergs melt

i love natre now
gods creations sweetly sing
in the breast of us

TWO THINGS HAIKU

i love rachel and
i love the planet with all
of the creatures here

BACK YARD HAIKU

jesus protect my swamp
of a back yard receding
into the heartland

BREATHING SPRING HAIKU

the purple and green
od our deep swampland and wood
lets morning breathe out

MODERN MORNINGS HAIKU

small flickers of light
from the computer herein
keeps us hypnotized

PORCH SILOUETTE HAIKU

shadows on the land
receding from this vista
of sunlight rising

PORCH SHADOW 2

the swampland back there
is dark and weedy messed up
the terror of heart

HELLO MORNING HAIKU

the dawn brings cheer here
the bird song on the lawn too
everyone giggles

NUTRIONAL HAIKU

the sweet greens of heat
the summer weeds of this time
nouishing our gut

NUTRIDRINK HAIKU

blend greens all up
raw greens in a drink instead
...liquid harmony

TWO HAIKU FOR LIGHT

light brilliant and pained
shivers from foliage on us
...our shadowed depths

the is a still life
...this landscape of coloring
on our flushed bent limbs

GHOSTS HAIKU

ghosts ricochet off
this shadowy morning chill
warning of the end

at the end of things
without god the oceans die
the waters boil up

we must cease this fat
gluttony of our passion
....cool and rest ourselves

MIGRAINE HAIKU

the zig zag lines come
and the rush of colored heat
then the skull splits here

afterwards there is
killer fatigue in the eyes
and body of it

and the fatigue lasts
several days of waiting
for zests returning

END DAYS HAIKU

what are end days now
are they a biblical end times
ormerely dumb facts

END DAYS 2

why do we call up
the end of our days on us
why do we cuase this

WAMPUM HAIKU

big fat money bags
loads of incredible cash
for the rich of us

STUPID WAMPUM

loads of idiot cash
lots of stupid thingss to buy
like labotomies

THREE SUMMER HAIKU

joes kid came down here
from the island to readand lrarn
our politics of greed

she reads frankenstein
for school and such an education
till the beast dies

cool breezees blow
against the climate warming
of the summer day

DOMESTC NATURE HAIKU

nature gt level
is the dark yard in the back
expanse of green porch

deer hide in our yard
in the wooded depths out here
they streak at night time

TV HAIKU

i watch tv too
to kill time, everything
dies somehow these days

nature will die and
most will not be on tv
....we will die softly

PRAYERS TO THE FORST HAIKU

love is in the swamp
sensual and young, or old
like decaying leaves

prayers to the forest
the trees eat oir refuse
and exhale pure air

GOD AND THE YARD HAIKU

god's nature call us
to renewal in hia heart
...the branches of the swamp

the voice of Jesus
echos in the forest now
and ever through us

HATRED HAIKU

how do we look down
on the soul of our time
the hatred...this age

why do people hate
what reason do we have now
to cast out people

FIVE SUMMER HAIKU

mother of jesus
in my deep lovely swampland
i look out to you

in the terrible
heat of global warming now
jesus still loves us

europe cooks hotter
the tides of history turn what
might be their ending

i love you rachel
more than god or anyone
...perhaps its a sin

i hope a cool world
has a happy endiing too
...i hope the kids do